THE ULTIMATE
MIAMI HEAT
TRIVIA BOOK

A Collection of Amazing Trivia Quizzes
and Fun Facts for Die-Hard Heat Fans!

Ray Walker

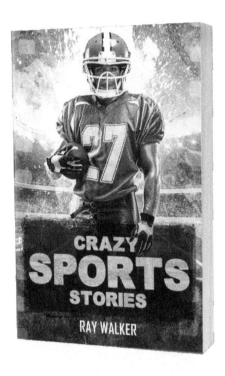

CONTENTS

INTRODUCTION

Team fandom should be inspirational. Our attachment to our favorite teams should fill us with pride, excitement, loyalty, and a sense of fulfillment in knowing that we are part of a community with many other fans who feel the same way.

Miami Heat fans are no exception. With a rich, successful history in the NBA, the Heat has inspired its supporters to strive for greatness through its tradition of colorful players, memorable eras, big moves, and unique moments.

This book is meant to be a celebration of those moments, and an examination of the collection of interesting, impressive, or important details that allow us to understand the full stories behind the players and the team.

You may use the book as you wish. Each chapter contains 20 quiz questions in a mixture of multiple-choice and true-false formats, an answer key (Don't worry, it's on a separate page!), and a section of 10 "Did You Know?" facts about the team.

Some will use it to test themselves with the quiz questions. How much Miami Heat history do you really know? How many of the finer points can you remember? Some will use it competitively (Isn't that the heart of sports?), waging contests with friends and fellow devotees to see who can lay claim to being the biggest fan. Some will enjoy it as a learning experience, gaining insight to enrich their fandom and add color to their understanding of their favorite team. Still others may use it to teach, sharing the wonderful anecdotes inside to inspire a new generation of fans to hop aboard the Heat bandwagon.

Whatever your purpose may be, we hope you enjoy delving into the amazing background of Miami Heat basketball!

Oh… for the record, information and statistics in this book are current up to the beginning of 2021. The Heat will surely topple more records and win more awards as the seasons pass, so keep this in mind when you're watching the next game with your friends, and someone starts a conversation with "Did you know…?".

CHAPTER 1:

ORIGINS & HISTORY

QUIZ TIME!

1. In which season did the Heat begin playing in the National Basketball Association?

    a. 1978-79
    b. 1988-89
    c. 1998-99
    d. 2008-09

2. The franchise was nearly called the Miami Marlins, partly to capitalize on alliteration and partly to honor the popular Florida fish. The name resurfaced decades later as the name of Miami's expansion team in Major League Baseball.

    a. True
    b. False

3. How was the nickname "Heat" chosen for the team?

a. It was chosen by team president Mark Silvestri and coincided with his sunglass company's name "Heat Vision."

b. It was recommended by NBA Commissioner David Stern and tied in with Florida's expansion team in the National Hockey League, the Tampa Bay Lightning.

c. It was the winning submission in a contest and referenced the city's warm climate.

d. It was selected by the ownership group, specifically to give the team the shortest nickname in the NBA.

4. In which season did the Heat begin to play in the new American Airlines Arena, their luxurious waterfront home on Biscayne Bay?

    a. 1996-97
    b. 1999-2000
    c. 2004-05
    d. 2017-18

5. Who was the founder of the Miami Heat?

    a. Larry O'Brien
    b. Micky Arison
    c. Pat Riley
    d. Ted Arison

6. In which season did the Heat earn its first playoff berth?

    a. 1988-89
    b. 1991-92
    c. 1995-96
    d. 1998-99

7. During the inaugural season, the Miami Heat lost its first 17 consecutive games, including a record-setting 47-point blowout loss to the Los Angeles Lakers.

   a. True
   b. False

8. How many times in franchise history has the Heat won a division title?

   a. 6
   b. 9
   c. 11
   d. 14

9. Who was the first Heat player ever to be named as Miami's representative in the NBA All-Star Game?

   a. Center Rony Seikaly
   b. Forward Glen Rice
   c. Center Alonzo Mourning
   d. Guard Dwyane Wade

10. Where does the Miami Heat rank among NBA franchises when it comes to most Larry O'Brien Championship Trophies won?

   a. 3rd place overall
   b. Tied for 6th place overall
   c. 8th place overall
   d. Tied for 13th place overall

11. How did the Heat fare in its 25th anniversary season in the NBA?

a. Lost the NBA championship against San Antonio Spurs

b. Won the NBA championship against the Dallas Mavericks

c. Lost the NBA championship against the Dallas Mavericks

d. Won the NBA championship against the San Antonio Spurs

12. The longest stretch the Heat has gone without making the playoffs is just three years, from 1988 to 1991, at the beginning of the franchise's existence.

a. True

b. False

13. Which team did Miami face in its first-ever NBA game (which resulted in a 111-91 Heat loss)?

a. Los Angeles Clippers

b. Orlando Magic

c. Charlotte Hornets

d. New Jersey Nets

14. Miami's top development team plays in the NBA G League. What is this team called?

a. Sioux Falls Skyforce

b. Little Havana Hoopheads

c. Dade Destroyers

d. Florida Sunshine

15. On November 5, 1988, which player scored the first basket in the first NBA game that the Miami Heat played?

    a. Center Rony Seikaly
    b. Guard Kevin Edwards
    c. Forward Grant Long
    d. Guard Rory Sparrow

16. As of 2020, Miami is tied with the Los Angeles Lakers and San Antonio Spurs as the NBA franchises that have sent the most players to the Summer Olympics to represent their countries.

    a. True
    b. False

17. How did Miami fare in its first-ever NBA playoff run?

    a. Lost in the first round to the Chicago Bulls
    b. Lost in the conference semifinals to the New York Knicks
    c. Lost in the conference finals to the Detroit Pistons
    d. Lost in the NBA Finals to the Dallas Mavericks

18. Which of the following teams did NOT join the NBA between 1988 and 1990 as an expansion franchise along with Miami?

    a. Charlotte Hornets
    b. Orlando Magic
    c. Minnesota Timberwolves
    d. Toronto Raptors

19. What is the name of the Heat mascot?

a. Shiner

b. Scorch

c. Burnie

d. Inferno

20. When new Heat owner Micky Arison lured coach Pat Riley away from the rival New York Knicks, the city of Miami threw a parade for Riley before he had ever coached a game for the Heat.

a. True

b. False

QUIZ ANSWERS

1. B – 1988-89

2. B – False

3. C – It was the winning submission in a team naming contest and referenced the city's warm climate.

4. B – 1999-2000

5. D – Ted Arison

6. B – 1991-92

7. A – True

8. D – 14

9. C – Center Alonzo Mourning

10. B – Tied for 6th place overall

11. D – Won the NBA championship against the San Antonio Spurs

12. A – True

13. A – Los Angeles Clippers

14. A – Sioux Falls Skyforce

15. D – Guard Rory Sparrow

16. B – False

17. A – Lost in the first round to the Chicago Bulls

18. D – Toronto Raptors

19. C – Burnie

20. A – True

DID YOU KNOW?

1. Despite being located on the East Coast of the United States, Miami was originally slotted into the NBA's Western Conference as part of their Midwest division. This awkward arrangement lasted only one season, and they have been in the Eastern Conference's Atlantic division or Southeast division ever since.

2. Although the Heat is Miami's premier basketball team, the area has also been home to a Continental Basketball Association team (the Miami Majesty) and an American Basketball Association team (the Miami Midnites).

3. When the United States selected Dream Team II, the assortment of players gathered for the 1994 World Championship, one Heat member made the cut: guard Steve Smith. In addition to Smith, though, four other Dream Teamers played for the Heat later: centers Alonzo Mourning and Shaquille O'Neal, swingman Dan Majerle, and guard Tim Hardaway.

4. While the Heat is an anchor tenant of the American Airlines Arena, that was not originally their exclusive home. The Women's National Basketball Association Miami Sol joined the Heat in the arena until the team folded in 2002. The arena also houses the Waterfront Theater, which seats up to 5,800 people for concerts or smaller events.

5. As a new team entering the NBA in 1988, the Heat paid a $32.5 million franchise fee for the right to join the league. For context, when the Toronto Raptors joined in 1993, they paid an expansion fee of $125 million.

6. The Heat's first playoff series victory came after the 1996-97 season, when they tasted sweet victory against their in-state rivals the Orlando Magic in a closely fought 3-2 series. They also dispatched the hated New York Knicks that year, 4-3, before bowing to the Chicago Bulls dynasty in the conference finals.

7. Miami's biggest NBA rival is generally thought to be the New York Knicks because the two teams faced each other for four consecutive years in the playoffs, from 1997 through 2000. The Knicks have the slight advantage in the head-to-head rivalry, at 65-61, but the Heat have won more championships as a franchise.

8. Animosity grew between the Heat and the Knicks during back-to-back playoff series in 1996-97 and 1997-98. New York starters Larry Johnson and John Starks were suspended for the deciding game of the first series, and Miami star Alonzo Mourning was suspended for the final game of the second series.

9. The first playoff sweep in which the Heat emerged victorious occurred in 1999-2000 when Miami claimed the second seed in the Eastern Conference and eliminated the seventh-seeded Detroit Pistons, three games to none.

10. In the beginning, the Heat struggled to find their footing and did not finish above eighth in their conference for the team's first eight years. However, in their ninth season, the team began a run of four straight years of finishing either first or second in the Eastern Conference.

CHAPTER 2:

JERSEYS & NUMBERS

QUIZ TIME!

1. When they began playing in the NBA in 1988, the Heat used what color scheme for their home and away uniforms?

   a. Red and white

   b. Red, orange, and yellow

   c. Teal and purple

   d. Black, white, red, and orange

2. The numbers 0 and 00 have been banned from circulation by Miami's ownership because they are seen to represent a losing attitude.

   a. True

   b. False

3. Which famous player had long been known by his jersey number by the time he joined Miami, and even starred in an Adidas commercial that referenced that number with

the memorable tagline: "That's me, employee number 8. I make baskets."?

    a. Center Isaac Austin

    b. Guard Shaun Livingston

    c. Guard Carlos Arroyo

    d. Forward Antoine Walker

4. The "Heat Strong" jerseys worn in 2015-16 used which color scheme to support a particular cause?

    a. Pink, white, and red to show support for breast cancer

    b. Camouflage and red to show support for soldiers in the military

    c. Red, white, and blue to show support for President Barack Obama's election

    d. Blue and black to show support for anti-bullying campaigns

5. Aside from the standard "Miami" or "Heat" wording, what else has been occasionally sported on the front of Heat jerseys?

    a. A green and orange "U," in tribute to the logo of the local University of Miami Hurricanes

    b. A special logo, featuring the shape of the state of Florida with a fire burning in the location of Miami

    c. The word "Champions" in seasons after the team had won the NBA title

    d. A silhouette of the Miami skyline with the Atlantic Ocean in the background

6. Which jersey number has proven to be most popular with Miami, having been worn by 14 different players?

    a. 5

    b. 9

    c. 11

    d. 21

7. The Heat retired superstar Michael Jordan's number 23, despite the fact that Jordan never played for the club.

    a. True

    b. False

8. Who is the player to wear the highest-numbered jersey in Heat franchise history?

    a. Guard Jason Williams

    b. Swingman Duncan Robinson

    c. Forward Jae Crowder

    d. Forward Brad Lohaus

9. Why did Heat guard Mario Chalmers choose to change his jersey number to 15 after giving up number 6 when superstar LeBron James came to Miami?

    a. He had worn the number in college previously, but it had been unavailable on the Heat when he arrived.

    b. He decided it was fitting because the digits worked mathematically: $1 + 5 = 6$.

    c. He chose it in honor of his mother, who had worn the number as a player as well.

    d. He made the choice for all of the reasons listed above.

10. Forward James Johnson is the only Heat player ever to wear which of the following uniform numbers?

    a. 8
    b. 16
    c. 24
    d. 32

11. Which unusual monochromatic color scheme has the Heat used occasionally as an alternate jersey?

    a. Pink, to celebrate Valentine's Day
    b. Orange, in tribute to Florida
    c. Green, to celebrate St. Patrick's Day
    d. White, as a fashion statement

12. Star center Alonzo Mourning is the only Heat player to have ever worn the number 33 on his jersey and will continue to be the only one as his number is now retired.

    a. True
    b. False

13. Why did franchise legend Dwyane Wade choose to wear number 3 on the back of his jersey?

    a. He was known as a three-point shooting specialist and loved to shoot from behind the arc.
    b. He chose it as a tribute to his father, Steven Wade, who wore the number decades before as a guard for the Philadelphia 76ers.

c. He wore it to remember three of his friends who were killed by gang violence in the city where Wade grew up with them.

d. He is a religious man and wore the number to represent the Holy Trinity of God the Father, the Son, and the Holy Ghost.

14. How many jersey numbers have the Miami Heat retired for their former players?

a. 2

b. 4

c. 5

d. 8

15. Which player competed for the Heat for just four seasons, the shortest tenure of anyone whose number has been retired by the franchise?

a. Center Shaquille O'Neal

b. Guard Tim Hardaway

c. Forward Chris Bosh

d. Center Alonzo Mourning

16. Five players have worn the number 1 for Miami, and every single one of them was a point guard.

a. True

b. False

17. Lucky number 7 has been worn by 11 Heat players over the years. Which athlete wore it for the longest time?

a. Forward Shawn Marion

b. Forward Lamar Odom

c. Center Jermaine O'Neal

d. Guard Goran Dragic

18. Who is the Heat player to have his number retired by the club most recently?

    a. Forward Chris Bosh

    b. Forward Udonis Haslem

    c. Guard Dwyane Wade

    d. Center Shaquille O'Neal

19. Which number did center Alonzo Mourning, who was named the first All-Star in Heat history, wear on the back of his jersey in that 1995-96 season?

    a. 3

    b. 11

    c. 20

    d. 33

20. More players have worn number 0 or 00 for Miami than have worn number 1.

    a. True

    b. False

QUIZ ANSWERS

1. D – Black, white, red, and orange

2. B – False

3. D – Forward Antoine Walker

4. B – Camouflage and red to show support for soldiers in the military

5. C – The word "Champions" in seasons after the team had won the NBA title

6. A – 5

7. A – True

8. C – Forward Jae Crowder

9. D – He made the choice for all of the reasons listed above.

10. B – 16

11. D – White, as a fashion statement

12. B – False

13. D – He is a religious man and wore the number to represent the Holy Trinity of God the Father, the Son, and the Holy Ghost.

14. C – 5

15. A – Center Shaquille O'Neal

16. B – False

17. D – Guard Goran Dragic

18. C – Guard Dwyane Wade

19. D – 33

20. A – True

DID YOU KNOW?

1. The Heat's logo, featuring a flaming basketball dropping through a basketball hoop, is not generally worn on the jerseys. However, the team has featured it occasionally when it is scheduled to play a game on Christmas Day.

2. Because of the incredible popularity of the Chicago Bulls' uniforms during the Michael Jordan era, several of Miami's jersey designs in the 1990s used similar elements and the same red, white, and black color scheme as Chicago.

3. On Latin nights, Miami celebrates the local culture of the city by wearing a jersey that features the wording "El Heat" across the chest.

4. Some numbers have proven unpopular with Miami players. Many numbers have gone unused in franchise history. No Heat player has ever worn a jersey with the following numbers: 18, 27, 29, 36, 37, 38, 39, 46, 47, or 48. In addition, the only number above 55 that has been used is 99, for one season by forward Jae Crowder.

5. In the rafters at American Airlines Arena hangs a Miami Heat jersey with the number 13. However, this number is not retired, nor hung to honor any member of the Heat. Instead, it was raised in tribute to quarterback Dan Marino of the National Football League's Miami Dolphins.

6. Miami has an entire series of alternate jerseys dubbed the "Vice Line," which takes inspiration from the baby blues and pinks used on the well-known 1980s TV series *Miami Vice*. This line includes "Sunset Vice," "Vice City," "Vice Wave," and "Vice Nights."

7. Superstition may have scared some Heat players away from wearing the number 13. Only seven players in franchise history have chosen it for themselves, and only center Bam Adebayo has kept the number for longer than three seasons.

8. No Heat player has ever worn a jersey with a number higher than 55 for longer than a single season before switching numbers or leaving the team.

9. One popular alternative jersey option used by the Heat is their "Floridian" uniform, which features two vertical stripes, one pink and one orange, running along the left side from shoulder to knee on both the jersey and the shorts. This is worn as an homage to the ABA's defunct Miami Floridians.

10. The Heat has used two jerseys, called "Back to Black" and "Black Tie," that were designed in a monochromatic black and white color scheme. Both versions featured the word "Miami" in the team's regular font across the front.

CHAPTER 3:

CATCHY NICKNAMES

QUIZ TIME!

1. Current Heat star Bam Adebayo is so commonly known as "Bam," that many Heat fans are unaware that his real name is which of the following?

   a. Bertram

   b. Daniel

   c. LaKeith

   d. Edrice

2. Dynamic Heat guard Tim Hardaway was often referred to as "Timmy Two-Step" thanks to the ball-handling skills that often faked opponents out of position.

   a. True

   b. False

3. The longtime home of the Heat, American Airlines Arena is also more commonly known by which popular nickname?

a. "The Airport"

b. "The Landing Pad"

c. "The Triple A"

d. "The Hothouse"

4. Which three young Miami Heat players were known as "The Baby Goat Gang" because of a celebration they used on the court that involved flashing their pinky fingers in the air?

   a. LeBron James, Dwyane Wade, and Chris Bosh

   b. Tim Hardaway, Voshon Lenard, and James Jones

   c. Rony Seikaly, Kevin Edwards, and Chris Gatling

   d. Tyler Herro, Kendrick Nunn, and Chris Silva

5. Why is Miami small forward Jimmy Butler nicknamed "Jimmy Buckets"?

   a. For his scoring prowess and ability to record points in many different ways

   b. For a task he performed as an NBA rookie, carrying buckets of Gatorade to and from the practice court

   c. For his tenacious defensive play and related third-person trash talk line, "Nobody gets buckets on Jimmy!"

   d. For a mispronunciation of his name by college coach Buzz Williams, which Butler used as motivation throughout his career

6. Where did Heat guard Vernell Eufaye Coles, more commonly known as "Bimbo," acquire his nickname?

a. From his tendency to forget details (such as peoples' names) quickly after hearing them

b. From an obscure country song that Coles's cousin had heard and mentioned in childhood

c. From his reputation as a ladies' man who did not believe in monogamy

d. From his low high school grades, which led to difficulty getting into college

7. Heat swingman Dan Majerle was such a forceful dunker that his thunderous slams earned him the frequently used nickname "Thunder Dan."

a. True

b. False

8. How was Heat guard Anfernee Hardaway given the nickname "Penny"?

a. His high school teammates called him that because he tucked a lucky penny into his sock before every game.

b. The media dubbed him "Penny" because in press conferences he spoke so little that "he'd never even give them his two cents on a subject."

c. His grandmother called him "Pretty" as a child, and, with her Southern accent, it sounded like "Penny."

d. His coach called him "Penny" because he "flipped so easily between offense and defense."

9. Which of the following is NOT a nickname that was given to Heat forward Lamar Odom while he was in the NBA?

a. "The Package"

b. "Candy Man"

c. "The Goods"

d. "O Damn"

10. Popular Heat forward "P.J." Brown's real given name(s) are which of the following?

a. Peter John

b. Patrick Joseph

c. Phillip Junior

d. Collier

11. Which Heat center was known to fans and teammates by the nickname "Big Z"?

a. Alonzo Mourning

b. Zydrunas Ilgauskas

c. Wang Zhizhi

d. KZ Okpala

12. After engaging in two memorable fights with his former Charlotte Hornets teammates as a newly traded member of the Miami Heat, ex-Hornets center Alonzo Mourning earned the nickname "The Vengeful Ex."

a. True

b. False

13. Which popular Heat player who was known to teammates by the nickname "Baby Jordan" took two NBA Slam Dunk contest titles, inspiring further comparisons to Chicago Bulls superstar Michael Jordan?

a. Forward Shawn Marion

b. Swingman Justise Winslow

c. Guard Harold Miner

d. Forward Hassan Whiteside

14. Which very confident Heat guard proclaimed in an interview that he was "the best shooter in the world," thus earning the tongue-in-cheek nickname "The World's Greatest Shooter" from other amused players?

a. Damon Jones

b. Eddie Jones

c. James Jones

d. Derrick Jones

15. Which Miami Heat player's name and shooting touch combined to develop into the nickname "G Money"?

a. Forward Brian Grant

b. Center Matt Geiger

c. Guard Gary Payton

d. Forward Glen Rice

16. Miami forward Udonis Haslem was called "Uncle Udo" by his young teammates because he was seen to provide leadership and playoff experience while demonstrating how to act as a professional athlete.

a. True

b. False

17. Which of the following qualities led Heat forward Chris Anderson to being given his nickname, "Birdman"?

a. His plethora of colorful tattoos

b. His impressive 84-inch wingspan

c. His ability to soar through the air for slam dunks

d. All of the above

18. Big man Chris Bosh toggled between power forward and center for the Heat, using his long, lanky frame in skillful ways that led to which animal nickname for him?

a. "The Bostrich"

b. "The Boshtopus"

c. "The Giraffe"

d. "Chrisanguatan"

19. Miami guard Goran Dragic was given a two-word nickname that utilizes his initials. Which of the following is it?

a. "General Defense"

b. "Gentle Destroyer"

c. "Gold Dragon"

d. "German Dracula"

20. Heat center Amar'e Stoudemire used an acronym as his preferred nickname. Stoudemire went by "STAT," which did not refer to statistics, as many assumed, but stood for "Standing Tall and Talented."

a. True

b. False

QUIZ ANSWERS

1. D – Edrice

2. B – False

3. C – "The Triple A"

4. D – Tyler Herro, Kendrick Nunn, and Chris Silva

5. A – For his scoring prowess and ability to record points in many different ways

6. B – From an obscure country song that Coles's cousin had heard and mentioned in childhood

7. A – True

8. C – His grandmother called him "Pretty" as a child, and, with her Southern accent, it sounded like "Penny."

9. D – "O Damn"

10. D – Collier

11. B – Zydrunas Ilgauskas

12. B – False

13. C – Guard Harold Miner

14. A – Damon Jones

15. D – Forward Glen Rice

16. B – False

17. D – All of the above

18. A – "The Bostrich"

19. C – "Gold Dragon"

20. A – True

DID YOU KNOW?

1. Swingman Joe Johnson had a short tenure with the Heat, at just 24 games, but he made a big impression in the nickname game. Johnson was variously known as "Iso Joe," "Big Shot Joe," "Joe Cool," and, most spectacularly, "Armadillo Cowboy."

2. Because coach Pat Riley left the Knicks on bad terms to become coach and team president of the Miami Heat, Knicks fans often referred to him as "Pat the Rat," helping to intensify Miami's biggest rivalry.

3. Miami's minority owner, Billy Cunningham, had a Hall of Fame basketball career in his own right and was nicknamed "The Kangaroo Kid" for his prowess in bouncing up and down to collect rebounds as a forward with the Philadelphia 76ers.

4. When Heat superstars Dwyane Wade, Chris Bosh, and LeBron James decided to play together in Miami, James dubbed the trio "The Heatles" because, just like legendary rock group The Beatles, they would "sell out arenas wherever they go."

5. While the Heat plays home games in the American Airlines Arena, the Dallas Mavericks take the court at the American Airlines Center. Twice in their history, the two teams have matched up in the NBA Finals, which were both commonly dubbed "The American Airlines Series."

6. When the Heat wore special "nickname" jerseys in 2014, allowing players to wear their nickname on the back of their jerseys instead of their usual surname, guard Ray Allen had one of the more popular entries. Allen wore "J. Shuttlesworth" on his back, a nod to the name of the character he played in the 1998 movie *He Got Game*.

7. The history of Heat center Shaquille O'Neal's nicknames is a long one. He has cycled through "Shaq," "Superman," "Diesel," "M.D.E." (Most Dominant Ever), "L.C.L." (Last Center Left), "Wilt Chamberneazy," "Osama Bin Shaq," "The Big Aristotle," "The Big Deporter," "The Big Felon," and "The Big Sidekick."

8. Heat point guard Rafer Alston had an unusual dribble and many ballhandling moves that were unorthodox and tricky to defend. Alston's skill and control with the ball led to his equally unusual nickname: "Skip to My Lou."

9. LeBron James was thought of as an all-time great basketball player while he was still in high school and, incredibly, only boosted his reputation through the years. By the time the forward arrived in Miami and led the team to multiple championships, he was already known by the well-earned nickname "King James."

10. Imposing power forward/center Kurt Thomas had a long career that began with Miami in 1995, ended in 2013, and included eight other teams in between. His nicknames evolved during his career. In the beginning, he was known as "Big Sexy" by those who liked him, and "Dirty

Kurt" by those who didn't. As he turned 40 years old in his last season, though, teammates took to calling him "Mid-Life" instead.

CHAPTER 4:

ALMA MATERS

QUIZ TIME!

1. Heat center Alonzo Mourning had a strong bond with players who attended his alma mater, Georgetown University. Which Hoya teammate offered to donate a kidney to Mourning, even going so far as to be tested to check his compatibility, when "Zo" needed a transplant?

   a. Center Dikembe Mutombo
   b. Center Patrick Ewing
   c. Guard Allen Iverson
   d. Forward Othella Harrington

2. The Heat has drafted more players from the Michigan State Spartans than from the Michigan Wolverines.

   a. True
   b. False

3. Guard Khalid Reeves played four years of college ball for which program before being drafted by the Heat?

a. Washington Huskies

b. Eastern Michigan Eagles

c. Arizona Wildcats

d. Cincinnati Bearcats

4. First-ever Miami Heat draft choice Rony Seikaly attended Syracuse University, where he played for the basketball team that went by which nickname?

a. Stampeders

b. Warriors

c. Pitbulls

d. Orangemen

5. From which of the following college basketball programs have the Heat drafted the most players?

a. Texas Christian Horned Frogs

b. Texas A&M Aggies

c. Texas Tech Red Raiders

d. Texas-El Paso Miners

6. Which famous college basketball coach did Heat point guard Rory Sparrow play for as a member of the Villanova Wildcats from 1976 to 1980?

a. John Wooden

b. Rick Pitino

c. Rollie Massimino

d. Mike Krzyzewski

7. Fan favorite guard Harold Miner is the only player ever selected by the Heat who played in college for the University of Southern California Trojans.

a. True

b. False

8. Forward P.J. Brown played four seasons for little-scouted Louisiana Tech University before starring with the Heat. What was his college team's nickname?

a. Heat
b. Wildcats
c. Bulldogs
d. Cajuns

9. The Heat selected two teammates from the Arizona Wildcats in the 1993 and 1994 NBA Drafts. Which teammates did they choose with those picks?

a. Center Ed Stokes and guard Khalid Reeves
b. Guard Steve Smith and center Matt Geiger
c. Forward Kurt Thomas and guard Charles Smith
d. Forward Jeff Webster and center Geoff Ackles

10. When professional players were finally allowed to participate in the Summer Olympics, in 1992, only one college player was selected for the American "Dream Team." Which future Miami Heat member was the chosen one?

a. Guard Steve Smith of the Michigan State Spartans
b. Center Alonzo Mourning of the Georgetown Hoyas
c. Forward Christian Laettner of the Duke Blue Devils
d. Forward Glen Rice of the Michigan Wolverines

11. How many Ivy League players have played for the Heat after being drafted by the franchise?

    a. 0

    b. 2

    c. 9

    d. 13

12. The Heat used the prep-to-pro method and drafted small forward Dorrell Wright directly out of high school in 2004.

    a. True

    b. False

13. Center Ken Johnson was drafted by the Heat out of what school that is better known as a football powerhouse than a basketball school?

    a. Louisiana State University

    b. University of Nebraska

    c. University of Alabama

    d. Clemson University

14. The Heat drafted only two players from the same school who went on to play more than 82 NBA games each for Miami. Who were these players?

    a. Forwards Wayne Simien and Michael Beasley of the Kansas Jayhawks

    b. Forward Willi Burton and swingman Rodney Buford of the Creighton Bluejays

c. Guard Eddie House and swingman Caron Butler of the Arizona State Sun Devils

d. Center Rony Seikaly and guard Sherman Douglas of the Syracuse Orangemen

15. The high-scoring Jimmy Butler was a member of which college squad before joining the Heat?

   a. UNLV Runnin' Rebels
   b. Texas Longhorns
   c. Marquette Golden Eagles
   d. Purdue Boilermakers

16. Forward Willie Burton, who was chosen 9th overall in 1990, is the highest-drafted player the Heat has ever selected from the University of Minnesota Golden Gophers.

   a. True
   b. False

17. In 1991-92, *Sports Illustrated* magazine considered four athletes for its college basketball player of the year award. All four of these players would spend time with the Miami Heat, but which won the award that year?

   a. Forward Christian Laettner of the Duke Blue Devils
   b. Center Shaquille O'Neal of the LSU Tigers
   c. Center Alonzo Mourning of the Georgetown Hoyas
   d. Guard Harold Miner of the USC Trojans

18. Two players were teammates in college with the Syracuse University Orangemen before taking the court together in Miami as well. Which two players were they?

a. Guard Harold Miner and forward Jeff Webster

b. Forwards Wayne Simien and Jarvis Varnado

c. Forward Nate Johnson and guard Scott Haffner

d. Center Rony Seikaly and guard Sherman Douglas

19. The high-scoring Dwyane Wade was a member of which college squad before his time on the court with the Heat?

a. University of North Carolina Tar Heels

b. University of Miami Hurricanes

c. Louisiana State University Tigers

d. Marquette University Golden Eagles

20. Due to their longstanding rivalry with the New York Knicks, Miami has never drafted a player who went to college in the state of New York.

a. True

b. False

QUIZ ANSWERS

1. B – Center Patrick Ewing

2. B – False

3. C – Arizona Wildcats

4. D – Orangemen

5. D – Texas-El Paso Miners

6. C – Rollie Massimino

7. B – False

8. C – Bulldogs

9. A – Center Ed Stokes and guard Khalid Reeves

10. C – Forward Christian Laettner of the Duke Blue Devils

11. A – 0

12. A – True

13. A – Louisiana State University

14. D – Center Rony Seikaly and guard Sherman Douglas of the Syracuse Orangemen

15. C – Marquette Golden Eagles

16. A – True

17. D – Guard Harold Miner of the USC Trojans

18. D – Center Rony Seikaly and guard Sherman Douglas

19. D – Marquette University Golden Eagles

20. B – False

DID YOU KNOW?

1. Guard Kevin Edwards, who led Miami in scoring during the team's first year in the NBA, played for the DePaul Blue Demons during his college days. After his NBA career ended, Edwards returned to his alma mater and became the director of community, corporate, and professional relations for DePaul's basketball team.

2. Miami has made two University of Kentucky Wildcats players top 15 picks in the NBA Draft. The team selected center Bam Adebayo 14th overall in 2017 and guard Tyler Herro 13th overall in 2019. The two never overlapped in college, as both entered the NBA Draft after their freshman seasons.

3. Two Heat players would reunite in Miami years after the youngsters starred for the fictional Western University Dolphins in the Hollywood film *Blue Chips*. Shaquille O'Neal played Dolphins center Neon Boudeaux and Anfernee Hardaway played guard Butch McRae, two college freshmen who were recruited to the school by accepting unethical financial contributions.

4. Forward Justise Winslow remains the only Duke University Blue Devil ever taken by the Miami Heat in an NBA Draft. Winslow was selected 10th overall in 2015.

5. Heat forward Juwan Howard was a member of "The Fab Five," a group of freshmen who led the Michigan University Wolverines to the NCAA finals in 1991-92. Twenty-eight years later, Howard returned to the school to become Michigan's head coach.

6. Heat forward Christian Laettner never quite reached the heights of his NCAA career in the NBA, though that would have been difficult. Laettner led the Duke Blue Devils to back-to-back NCAA championships in 1991 and 1992, winning Final Four Most Outstanding Player in 1991, and being named an All-American in both years.

7. The most players Miami has drafted from any school is three, from the University of Memphis Tigers. These selections were bookended by forwards Sylvester Gray, who was chosen in the team's first NBA Draft, in 1988, and Precious Achiuwa, who was taken in 2020, the team's most recent draft.

8. Forward Michael Beasley was "one and done" at Kansas State University before he was drafted by the Heat, but it was quite the "one." Beasley finished with the second-most rebounds ever grabbed by an NCAA freshman and the third most points, and he set over 30 Kansas State records as well.

9. Center Ernest Brown was lucky to be noticed by NBA scouts. Brown played at Indian Hills Community College, a school that does not traditionally receive much attention from NBA teams.

10. The Heat have drafted one player from the University of Miami Hurricanes: small forward Tim James in the 1st round of the 1999 NBA Draft. James did see the court for the Heat, only playing in four games with the team and 43 overall in the NBA before his career finished.

CHAPTER 5:

STATISTICALLY SPEAKING

QUIZ TIME!

1. What is Miami's franchise record for most victories in a single regular season?

   a. 54
   b. 58
   c. 61
   d. 66

2. No one in Heat history is within 2,000 assists of guard Dwyane Wade at the top of Miami's record book.

   a. True
   b. False

3. Four players have recorded over 4,000 career rebounds for the Heat. Which one of them has the most?

   a. Center Alonzo Mourning
   b. Center Rony Seikaly
   c. Forward Udonis Haslem
   d. Guard Dwyane Wade

4. Who is the Heat single-season leader in points scored, with 2,386?

   a. Forward Glen Rice
   b. Forward LeBron James
   c. Guard Dwyane Wade
   d. Center Shaquille O'Neal

5. Which Heat player really made his shots count, compiling Miami's highest career shooting percentage?

   a. Center Hassan Whiteside
   b. Center Shaquille O'Neal
   c. Center Matt Geiger
   d. Center Jermaine O'Neal

6. The most personal fouls committed in a season by a Heat player is 337. Which aggressive player established this club record?

   a. Center Alonzo Mourning
   b. Center Brian Grant
   c. Center Rony Seikaly
   d. Forward Grant Long

7. Guard Dwyane Wade has attempted more than double the number of career free throws for the Heat as center Alonzo Mourning, who is in second place on the franchise list.

   a. True
   b. False

8. Which player holds the Miami record for most blocks in a single season, with 294?

   a. Center Hassan Whiteside
   b. Center Bam Adebayo
   c. Center Shaquille O'Neal
   d. Center Alonzo Mourning

9. Which Heat player has played the most NBA games with the franchise?

   a. Guard Dwyane Wade
   b. Forward Udonis Haslem
   c. Guard Mario Chalmers
   d. Center Rony Seikaly

10. The talented Dwyane Wade is Miami's all-time leader with how many points?

   a. 15,633
   b. 18,840
   c. 21,556
   d. 25,307

11. Guard Dwyane Wade holds the single-season Heat record for points per game. How many points did he average per game during that 2008-09 season?

   a. 25.8
   b. 27.3
   c. 29.5
   d. 30.2

12. Guard Dwyane Wade has *missed* more field goals during his Heat career than any other Miami player has even *attempted.*

    a. True
    b. False

13. Which Heat shooter sank the most free throws while playing with the club?

    a. Guard Dwyane Wade
    b. Forward LeBron James
    c. Center Rony Seikaly
    d. Guard Eddie Jones

14. How many times does franchise icon Dwyane Wade's name appear on the Heat's top 10 list for points scored by a player in a season?

    a. 2
    b. 4
    c. 5
    d. 7

15. How many Heat players have taken over 5,000 field goal attempts for the club during their careers?

    a. 1
    b. 3
    c. 5
    d. 9

16. Sharpshooter Tim Hardaway hit 203 three-pointers during the 1996-97 season, which remains a franchise record.

a. True

b. False

17. Which Miami shooter recorded the highest career three-point shooting percentage with the Heat, with .490 percent made?

   a. Swingman Dan Majerle

   b. Swingman Jason Kapono

   c. Guard Jon Sundvold

   d. Guard Ray Allen

18. Which Heat player recorded the most rebounds in one season for the team by grabbing 1,088, marking the only time someone from the franchise has cracked 1,000?

   a. Center Rony Seikaly

   b. Forward Hassan Whiteside

   c. Forward Brian Grant

   d. Center Shaquille O'Neal

19. Which two teammates posted the highest combined steals total in a season for the Heat, snatching 333 balls away from their opponents?

   a. Guards Kevin Edwards and Sherman Douglas

   b. Guards Tim Hardaway and Bimbo Coles

   c. Guards Dwyane Wade and Mario Chalmers

   d. Guard Tim Hardaway and center Alonzo Mourning

20. Coach Erik Spoelstra's 2012-13 season is the benchmark in terms of winning percentage, as he led the team to a .805 winning percentage in the regular season.

a. True
b. False

QUIZ ANSWERS

1. D – 66

2. A – True

3. C – Forward Udonis Haslem

4. C – Guard Dwyane Wade

5. B – Center Shaquille O'Neal

6. D – Forward Grant Long

7. B – False

8. D – Center Alonzo Mourning

9. A – Guard Dwyane Wade

10. C – 21,556

11. D – 30.2

12. A – True

13. A – Guard Dwyane Wade

14. C – 5

15. D – 9

16. B – False

17. B – Swingman Jason Kapono

18. B – Forward Hassan Whiteside

19. C – Guards Dwyane Wade and Mario Chalmers

20. A – True

DID YOU KNOW?

1. Four players have scored more than 7,000 points with the Heat franchise. Forwards LeBron James and Glen Rice and center Alonzo Mourning accomplished the feat, but all three are at least 10,000 points behind franchise leader Dwyane Wade, who has 21,556.

2. Heat icon LeBron James ranks third on the all-time list for most points scored in the history of the NBA. James trails only Kareem Abdul-Jabbar of the Los Angeles Lakers and Karl Malone of the Utah Jazz. Both Abdul-Jabbar and Malone are retired, while James remains active and has a chance to take the lead eventually.

3. The incomparable Dwyane Wade still stands as the player who has contributed to the most victories in team history. Wade accumulated 116.1 win shares during his career, almost double that of superstar LeBron James, who is second in Miami's history.

4. Center Alonzo Mourning was a force in the paint for the Heat, blocking 1,625 shots during his Miami career to lead the franchise in that statistic. This is almost exactly double the total of guard Dwyane Wade, who is second in team history with 812.

5. Only two NBA players have ever led their team in points, steals, blocks, rebounds, and assists during an NBA final series. Heat forward Jimmy Butler accomplished this in a

losing effort during the 2020 championships. LeBron James also managed to do so but that was in 2016, after James had left the Heat to play for the Cleveland Cavaliers.

6. Power forward Udonis Haslem sits alone atop all of the Heat's rebounding records. Haslem pulled down 1,607 offensive boards and 4,147 defensive ones for 5,754 total rebounds with Miami.

7. Forwards LeBron James and Anthony Mason hold the top spots in the Heat record books in minutes per game. The indefatigable LeBron James averaged 38 minutes per game during his Heat career, but Mason had the most impressive season, averaging 40.7 minutes a night in 2000-01.

8. The most recent time the Heat sank more than 900 three-pointers in a season was 2019-20 when they set a franchise record by draining 979. This marked the fourth consecutive year that Miami had notched a new franchise record in three-pointers made.

9. The deadliest Heat shooter on the free-throw line was guard Ray Allen. He shot a team-record .894 from the stripe, .11% better than guard Jason Williams, who is second on the list.

10. In 2008-09, star guard Dwyane Wade had the green light and fired 1,739 shots, which established the Heat record for most shots taken by one player in a single season. He scored 854 times, which was good for a .491 shooting percentage and the NBA scoring title.

CHAPTER 6:

THE TRADE MARKET

QUIZ TIME!

1. One of Miami's first trades occurred on June 23, 1988, when the Heat received a 2nd round draft choice from the Milwaukee Bucks. Which player did they give up in return?

   a. Center Fred Roberts
   b. Forward Glenn Robinson
   c. Guard Dell Curry
   d. Guard Tim Hardaway

2. Miami has never in its history completed a trade with the San Antonio Spurs.

   a. True
   b. False

3. Although iconic Heat guard Dwyane Wade played 13 seasons with the team after they drafted him, Miami had to reacquire him in a 2018 trade, allowing Wade to retire with the Heat. From which team did they reacquire Wade?

a. Chicago Bulls

b. Cleveland Cavaliers

c. Los Angeles Lakers

d. Toronto Raptors

4. A 2011 1ˢᵗ round draft pick that was eventually used on center Jonas Valanciunas was acquired by Miami from the Toronto Raptors in 2009. Miami traded the pick back to Toronto in 2010. Which of the following players was NOT involved in either deal featuring that draft pick?

a. Center Jermaine O'Neal

b. Forward Shawn Marion

c. Forward Chris Bosh

d. Guard Kyle Lowry

5. Which useful Heat player was NOT sent to the New Orleans Pelicans in a three-team trade in 2015 but moved instead to the Phoenix Suns in the same deal?

a. Forward Shawne Williams

b. Guard Norris Cole

c. Forward Danny Granger

d. Center Justin Hamilton

6. One of the Heat's best trades saw them acquire swingman Jimmy Butler in a four-team deal in 2019. Which team regretted making that deal with Miami after Butler led the Heat to the NBA Finals the following year?

a. Los Angeles Clippers

b. Philadelphia 76ers

c. Minnesota Timberwolves

d. Portland Trail Blazers

7. Miami has completed more trades with the Cleveland Cavaliers than with any other NBA franchise.

a. True

b. False

8. Which players did the Heat give up to pry popular center Alonzo Mourning away from the Charlotte Hornets in 1995?

a. Forward Glen Rice and center Matt Geiger

b. Center Rony Seikaly and forward Matt Bonner

c. Forward Jamal Mashburn and guard David Wesley

d. Guard Bobby Phills and center Elden Campbell

9. Miami's director of player personnel, Chris Wallace, was effectively traded to which team in 1997, with the Heat receiving a 2nd round pick in return?

a. New Jersey Nets

b. Atlanta Hawks

c. Sacramento Kings

d. Boston Celtics

10. Whom did the Miami Heat select with the 1992 draft pick traded to the team from the Los Angeles Lakers in exchange for the Heat selecting forward Billy Thompson in the 1988 Expansion Draft?

a. Forward Glen Rice

b. Center Matt Geiger

c. Guard Alvin Robertson

d. Center Chris Gatling

11. Which of the following Hall of Fame players did NOT retire with the Miami Heat, but was instead dealt away in a trade?

 a. Guard Ray Allen

 b. Center Alonzo Mourning

 c. Center Shaquille O'Neal

 d. Guard Gary Payton

12. Due to their close proximity, Miami has never in its history completed a trade with the other NBA team from Florida, the Orlando Magic.

 a. True

 b. False

13. Which player did the Heat acquire from the Golden State Warriors along with star point guard Tim Hardaway in a successful 1995 trade?

 a. Center Chris Gatling

 b. Center Kevin Willis

 c. Guard Bimbo Coles

 d. Guard Voshon Lenard

14. To which team and for whom did the Heat trade guard Rory Sparrow, who had scored the first points in Miami's franchise history?

 a. To the Philadelphia 76ers for forwards David Roberts and Mike McNally

b. To the Sacramento Kings for guard Bimbo Coles

c. To the Portland Trail Blazers for guard Norris Cole

d. To the Utah Jazz for center Mark Eaton and forward Walt Williams

15. From which team did the Heat acquire useful forward Jamal Mashburn in a lopsided 1997 swap?

   a. Houston Rockets
   b. Charlotte Hornets
   c. Indiana Pacers
   d. Dallas Mavericks

16. In a trade that worked out well for Miami in 2015, the Heat acquired not just point guard Goran Dragic, who remains with the team, from the Phoenix Suns, but also his brother Zoran Dragic, a shooting guard who played just 10 games for Miami.

   a. True
   b. False

17. When the Heat needed to trade star center Shaquille O'Neal away in 2008, which franchise did they send him to in order to get the two-player return that they wanted?

   a. Boston Celtics
   b. Cleveland Cavaliers
   c. Los Angeles Lakers
   d. Phoenix Suns

18. Which player did Miami NOT give up in return after acquiring former 1ˢᵗ overall pick Shaquille O'Neal from the Los Angeles Lakers in 2004?

    a. Swingman Caron Butler
    b. Guard Eddie Jones
    c. Forward Brian Grant
    d. Forward Lamar Odom

19. In 2000, the Heat completed a large three-team trade, acquiring popular forward Brian Grant. The team sent out forwards Chris Gatling, Clarence Weatherspoon and a 1ˢᵗ round pick. Who were the other two teams involved in the complicated deal?

    a. Golden State Warriors and Denver Nuggets
    b. Philadelphia 76ers and New Jersey Nets
    c. Portland Trail Blazers and Cleveland Cavaliers
    d. New York Knicks and Orlando Magic

20. Miami general manager Randy Pfund once proposed a deal to the Chicago Bulls that would have sent Miami icon Rony Seikaly to the Windy City in exchange for a young Michael Jordan.

    a. True
    b. False

QUIZ ANSWERS

1. A – Center Fred Roberts

2. A – True

3. B – Cleveland Cavaliers

4. D – Guard Kyle Lowry

5. C – Forward Danny Granger

6. B – Philadelphia 76ers

7. A – True

8. A – Forward Glen Rice and center Matt Geiger

9. D – Boston Celtics

10. B – Center Matt Geiger

11. C – Center Shaquille O'Neal

12. B – False

13. A – Center Chris Gatling

14. B – To the Sacramento Kings for guard Bimbo Coles

15. D – Dallas Mavericks

16. A – True

17. D – Phoenix Suns

18. B – Guard Eddie Jones

19. C – Portland Trail Blazers and Cleveland Cavaliers

20. B – False

DID YOU KNOW?

1. Miami has never sent an actual player to the Chicago Bulls. They have made two trades with Chicago, acquiring one 2nd round draft choice that was later used to select Tommy Smith and a conditional pick that did not convey.

2. The Miami Heat and New York Knicks have had a fairly heated rivalry throughout their existence, particularly during the 1990s. The two teams have set aside their dislike for each other to make a trade only once in Miami's long tenure in the NBA. Even that deal was a bit forced, since it was caused by Miami signing away Knicks coach Pat Riley and New York filing a grievance.

3. One of the larger trades in Miami history occurred in 2005 and involved a whopping five teams. Miami got together with the Boston Celtics, Utah Jazz, New Orleans Hornets, and Memphis Grizzlies on a massive swap that moved 13 players and two draft picks. Miami was heavily represented in the deal, as they brought in Antoine Walker, Jason Williams, Roberto Duenas, Andre Emmett, and James Posey.

4. Miami and the Charlotte Hornets have a rich history of trades. Significant names moved between the two teams include centers Alonzo Mourning and Matt Geiger; forwards Glen Rice, P.J. Brown, Jamal Mashburn, Anthony

61

Mason, and Otis Thorpe; and guards Eddie Jones, Ricky Davis, Dale Ellis, and Steve Smith.

5. Bringing in a veteran big man was a priority for the Heat in 1992, and they accomplished it in a trade for John Salley from the Detroit Pistons. Salley played well for Miami, but the better end of the deal went to Detroit, who used the draft pick they gained on guard Lindsey Hunter. Hunter excelled for 12 seasons with the Pistons.

6. In October 2007, Miami acquired center Mark Blount from the Minnesota Timberwolves. Two years later, Miami shipped him back to Minnesota in return for guard Quentin Richardson.

7. One of the worst trades made by the Heat occurred in 1994 when they sent forward Grant Long, guard Steve Smith, and a 2nd round draft pick to the Atlanta Hawks for center Kevin Willis and a 1st round draft choice. Willis played parts of just two seasons for the Heat, while Smith starred for five years in Atlanta.

8. The Heat definitely hasn't mined the New Jersey Nets for talent in player swaps. In the only deal ever made between the two teams, Miami traded guard Chris Quinn to New Jersey in 2010 for essentially nothing (a 2nd round draft choice that never conveyed because it was protected). The two teams never made a swap again.

9. In a deal that was very unpopular at the time, Miami dealt original Heat center Rony Seikaly in 1994. The Heat wanted to change up their roster and sent Seikaly to

Golden State, despite the impassioned pleas of fans. Neither Billy Owens nor Sasha Danilovic, received in exchange, was a star, but the trade still worked out okay for Miami.

10. One of the largest and most impactful trades ever made by the Heat was completed July 10, 2010, with the Cleveland Cavaliers. Miami sent four draft picks to Cleveland and received superstar forward LeBron James in the blockbuster trade. James led the Heat to their most successful era with four straight NBA Finals appearances and two championships.

CHAPTER 7:

DRAFT DAY

QUIZ TIME!

1. Which prospect did the Heat select with the franchise's first-ever draft choice in 1988?

   a. Guard Kevin Edwards
   b. Center Rony Seikaly
   c. Forward Grant Long
   d. Forward Glen Rice

2. The Heat has never held the 1st overall pick in the NBA Draft in the entire history of the franchise.

   a. True
   b. False

3. How high did Miami select power forward Grant Long in the 1988 NBA Entry Draft when the team chose players for its inaugural season?

   a. 1st round, 5th overall
   b. 2nd round, 33rd overall

c. 3rd round, 74th overall

d. 7th round, 222nd overall

4. Which point guard did the Heat select highest in the NBA Entry Draft, using the 5th overall draft pick?

a. Bimbo Coles

b. Khalid Reeves

c. Tim Hardaway

d. Dwyane Wade

5. Who was the first player ever selected by the Heat in the NBA Entry Draft to be the franchise's lone selection for a single year?

a. Guard Steve Smith in 1991

b. Forward Glen Rice in 1989

c. Center Ed Stokes in 1993

d. Center Ken Johnson in 2001

6. Which player, drafted by the Heat, went on to score the most NBA points for another team (10,606) after leaving Miami?

a. Guard Steve Smith

b. Forward Glen Rice

c. Forward Kurt Thomas

d. Forward Caron Butler

7. Miami has drafted a player who played only a single game in the NBA, but power forward Jerome Beasley played only two NBA games, scoring two points in his short career.

a. True

b. False

8. The Heat have looked to Europe for talent very infrequently in the NBA Entry Draft and have selected only two players from European nations, rather than the American college system (both times trading these players on draft day). Which nations were these two players from?

a. France and Serbia

b. Croatia and Bosnia and Herzegovina

c. Bulgaria and Italy

d. Greece and Germany

9. Fan favorite Sherman Douglas was selected in the 2nd round by the Miami Heat in 1989. Which position did he play?

a. Point guard

b. Small forward

c. Power forward

d. Center

10. When the NBA welcomed the Heat in 1988, some teams were worried about losing players in the resulting dispersal draft. The Los Angeles Lakers were one such team, and they sent a 2nd round draft choice to Miami so that the Heat would not select which of the following players?

a. Guard Magic Johnson

b. Forward James Worthy

c. Center Vlade Divac

d. Center Kareem Abdul-Jabbar

11. Similarly, the Boston Celtics sent a 2nd round draft choice to Miami so that the Heat would not select which of the following players?

a. Center Robert Parish

b. Forward Dino Radja

c. Guard Dennis Johnson

d. Guard Danny Ainge

12. Three times during the 2010s, Miami traded away all of its draft picks or selected players on draft day.

a. True

b. False

13. The Heat struck out mightily in the 2010 NBA Draft, selecting four players who scored a total of how many points in the NBA?

a. 0

b. 58

c. 223

d. 509

14. At which of the draft spots in the top 10 in the NBA Draft has Miami selected more than any other?

a. 2nd overall

b. 5th overall

c. 9th overall

d. 10th overall

15. Talented forward Michael Beasley was drafted by Miami 2nd overall in the 2008 NBA Entry Draft. Which excellent player was selected ahead of him?

    a. Forward Kevin Love by the Memphis Grizzlies
    b. Point guard Derrick Rose by the Chicago Bulls
    c. Forward Blake Griffin by the Los Angeles Clippers
    d. Point guard Russell Westbrook by the Seattle SuperSonics

16. Forward Glen Rice was such a talented athlete coming out of college that he was drafted in not one but three sports (basketball, baseball, and football).

    a. True
    b. False

17. Up to and including the 2020 NBA Entry Draft, how many player selections has the Miami Heat made in franchise history?

    a. 19
    b. 32
    c. 58
    d. 93

18. How many times in history has Miami used a top-10 overall draft pick?

    a. 3
    b. 7
    c. 9
    d. 16

19. What is the lowest position in the draft that the Heat have selected a player who would go on to make the Naismith Memorial Basketball Hall of Fame?

    a. 1st round, 3rd overall
    b. 1st round, 19th overall
    c. 2nd round, 37th overall
    d. The Heat has never drafted a player who was elected to the Hall of Fame.

20. There have been 26 players in the NBA who measured 7'3" or taller. The Heat has never drafted any of them.

    a. True
    b. False

QUIZ ANSWERS

1. B – Center Rony Seikaly

2. A – True

3. B – 2nd round, 33rd overall

4. D – Dwyane Wade

5. C – Center Ed Stokes in 1993

6. D – Forward Caron Butler

7. A – True

8. B – Croatia and Bosnia and Herzegovina

9. A – Point guard

10. D – Center Kareem Abdul-Jabbar

11. C – Guard Dennis Johnson

12. A – True

13. C – 223

14. D – 10th overall

15. B – Point guard Derrick Rose by the Chicago Bulls

16. B – False

17. C – 58

18. C – 9

19. D – The Heat has never drafted a player who was elected to the Hall of Fame.

20. A – True

DID YOU KNOW?

1. Between 2002 and 2004, Miami enjoyed a stretch of selecting at least one player each year who lasted 500 or more games in the NBA. During those years, they chose Caron Butler, Dorell Wright, Dwyane Wade, and Rasual Butler.

2. In 2002, the Heat went all in on Butlers, selecting swingmen Caron Butler in the 1st round and Rasual Butler in the 2nd round. The two men were not related but became friends during their two seasons with the Heat before Caron was traded to the Los Angeles Lakers and Rasual was sent to the New Orleans Hornets.

3. Of all the players drafted in Miami history, big man Kurt Thomas leads in games played (1,110) and rebounds (7,328), although Thomas stayed with the Heat for just 92 of those games and collecting 546 of those boards with the franchise.

4. Ironically, the Heat did not draft its biggest hometown star. Power forward Udonis Haslem was born in Miami and has spent an incredible 17 seasons with the team, but he signed with them as an undrafted free agent in 2003.

5. The first Heat draft pick who played 1,000 NBA games was power forward Grant Long out of Eastern Michigan University. Long played nearly half of his 1,003 career

games in Miami before bouncing around between Atlanta, Vancouver, Memphis, Detroit, and Boston.

6. Miami has a thing for round numbers. The team has held the 10th, 20th, and 40th overall picks three times each, more than any other spot in the draft. Also tied with three times is the 53rd overall selection, which breaks the round number pattern, but did yield useful players Rasual Butler and Rodney Buford.

7. The largest Miami draft class ever was selected in the Heat's first year, 1988, when the team drafted six players. All of those players suited up in the NBA and half of them (Rony Seikaly, Kevin Edwards, and Grant Long) carved out long-lasting careers.

8. When the Heat and the Charlotte Hornets entered the NBA in 1988, a coin flip was held to determine draft order. Charlotte won, and elected to take the higher pick in the rookie draft. This left Miami with the first pick in the Expansion Draft, where they chose center Arvid Kramer from the Dallas Mavericks. Kramer had previously been selected by the Mavericks from the Denver Nuggets in the 1980 Expansion Draft as well.

9. The player chosen by Miami in the team's Expansion Draft in 1988 who lasted the longest with the team was guard Jon Sundvold. Sundvold played with the Heat from 1988 to 1992.

10. The 2003 NBA Draft is often cited as one of the best and deepest drafts in history, and nobody benefitted more

from it than the Miami Heat. At one point, the Heat had three of the top five selections in the draft on their team: 1st overall selection LeBron James, 4th overall pick Chris Bosh, and 5th overall choice Dwyane Wade.

CHAPTER 8:

THE GUARDS

QUIZ TIME!

1. Which point guard played more minutes than any other for Miami during the team's challenging first season in the NBA in 1988-89, suiting up for 80 games and finishing second on the team in scoring?

   a. Pearl Washington
   b. Kevin Edwards
   c. Rory Sparrow
   d. Craig Neal

2. Miami point guard Mario Chalmers set the team record for most steals in a single game (9) in only his fourth career NBA contest.

   a. True
   b. False

3. Which point guard has recorded the most career turnovers while with the Miami Heat?

a. Tim Hardaway

b. Mario Chalmers

c. Goran Dragic

d. Dwyane Wade

4. Which guard has played more minutes in the Heat lineup than anyone else?

a. Dwyane Wade

b. Mario Chalmers

c. Tim Hardaway

d. Eddie Jones

5. Undrafted Heat guard Kendrick Nunn accomplished all of the following feats during his rookie season in 2019-20 except for which one?

a. Being the first undrafted rookie to notch more than one Rookie of the Month award

b. Breaking a 50-year-old record for most points by an undrafted rookie in his first five games

c. Passing for more assists than any undrafted rookie in NBA history

d. Becoming the quickest Heat rookie ever to record 500 career points

6. In his rookie season, guard Eddie House married his wife, who is the sister of which of his Miami Heat teammates?

a. Center Hassan Whiteside

b. Forward Udonis Haslem

c. Guard Dwyane Wade

d. Guard Mike Bibby

7. It is a Heat tradition for every point guard to lob an alley-oop for each teammate during the warm-up before a home playoff game.

   a. True
   b. False

8. Which of the following facts about Heat shooting guard Eddie Jones is NOT true?

   a. He appeared on the cover of the video game *NBA Shootout '97*.
   b. He appeared as a college professor in a music video by the rap group 2 Live Crew.
   c. He appeared in an episode of *Pros vs. Joes* where he competed against ordinary athletes.
   d. He appeared in a Taco Bell commercial that featured center Shaquille O'Neal dealing with "Taco Neck Syndrome."

9. Which Heat guard scored the most ever points by a reserve (32) in a 136-130 double-overtime victory over the Orlando Magic?

   a. Voshon Lenard
   b. Brian Shaw
   c. Tyler Johnson
   d. Derek Anderson

10. Point guard Goran Dragic recorded his second career NBA triple-double (and first with the Heat) against which NBA team on March 28, 2019?

a. Phoenix Suns

b. New Orleans Pelicans

c. Dallas Mavericks

d. Houston Rockets

11. Heat mainstay Bimbo Coles played over 450 NBA games with the club. Where does he rank in career games played for Miami?

a. 1st overall

b. 3rd overall

c. 5th overall

d. 8th overall

12. Guard Eddie House began and ended his NBA career with the Miami Heat after playing for eight different franchises in eight years between those stints.

a. True

b. False

13. Which of the following positions has popular former Heat guard Anfernee Hardaway NOT held after retiring from his playing career?

a. Part owner of the Memphis Grizzlies, along with musician Justin Timberlake and quarterback Peyton Manning

b. State senator for the Republican Party in the state of Tennessee, who has been elected three times

c. Owner of a beauty salon located in downtown Memphis

d. Head coach of the University of Memphis Tigers men's basketball team

14. Which of these current Heat guards has been with the team for seven seasons, the longest current tenure in Miami's backcourt?

   a. Goran Dragic
   b. Avery Bradley
   c. Tyler Herro
   d. Kendrick Nunn

15. Which of the following facts about Heat point guard Bimbo Coles's athletic prowess is NOT true?

   a. Coles made All-American as a high school football player.
   b. Coles was drafted by Major League Baseball's Philadelphia Phillies.
   c. Coles was drafted by Major League Baseball's California Angels.
   d. Coles was offered a wrestling scholarship to Iowa University.

16. Former Heat point guard Mario Chalmers was the first guard in team history to hit a three-pointer, which did not occur until Miami's second NBA game, in October 1988.

   a. True
   b. False

17. Which of the following is NOT a fact about Miami Heat guard Tyler Herro?

a. A rookie poll voted Herro the best shooter in the 2019 NBA Draft class.

b. Herro has a song named after him, recorded by musician Jack Harlow.

c. Herro arrived at his contract signing at American Airlines Arena on a jet ski.

d. Herro was the first player born after the 1990s to participate in an NBA final.

18. Miami point guard Tim Hardaway played alongside teammate Alonzo Mourning for America in the 2000 Summer Olympics, which was held in which city?

a. Atlanta, Georgia

b. Athens, Greece

c. Beijing, China

d. Sydney, Australia

19. Longtime Heat point guard Mario Chalmers is the only player born in which state ever to play in the NBA?

a. Alaska

b. Delaware

c. Hawaii

d. Utah

20. Heat guard Tim Hardaway set an interesting record by recording 39 consecutive assists to the same player (teammate Alonzo Mourning).

a. True

b. False

QUIZ ANSWERS

1. C – Rory Sparrow

2. A – True

3. D – Dwyane Wade

4. A – Dwyane Wade

5. C – Passing for more assists than any undrafted rookie in NBA history

6. D – Guard Mike Bibby

7. B – False

8. B – He appeared as a college professor in a music video by the rap group 2 Live Crew.

9. C – Tyler Johnson

10. C – Dallas Mavericks

11. D – 8th overall

12. A – True

13. B – State senator for the Republican Party in the state of Tennessee, who has been elected three times

14. A – Goran Dragic

15. D – Coles was offered a wrestling scholarship to Iowa University.

16. B – False

17. C – Herro arrived at his contract signing at American Airlines Arena on a jet ski.

18. D – Sydney, Australia

19. A – Alaska

20. B – False

DID YOU KNOW?

1. The Heat's first point guard, Rory Sparrow, signed with the team as a free agent before the team's inaugural season, knowing that he would receive a lot of playing time. In the process, Sparrow went from backing up superstar Michael Jordan on a Chicago Bulls team that won 50 games the year before to a Heat team that finished an NBA worst 15-67.

2. Miami guard Brian Shaw was well liked in the locker room and the player that Heat center Shaquille O'Neal called his most respected NBA teammate. Shaw would throw alley-oop passes for O'Neal, a combination dubbed "The Shaw-Shaq Redemption." The duo played together in Orlando and Los Angeles but never overlapped in Miami.

3. The $2.5 million donation made by former Heat guard Steve Smith to Michigan State University in 1997 was, at the time, the highest single amount ever donated by an athlete to his alma mater. The money was used to help pay for the Clara Bell Smith Student Athlete Academic Center (in honor of Smith's mother) and to fund the Steve Smith Scholarship for Academic Achievement.

4. After being selected by the Heat in the 1988 NBA Expansion Draft, guard Jon Sundvold posted the highest

three-point shooting percentage in the league in 1989, making 52.2% of his long-range attempts.

5. While Miami guard Dion Waiters had some success on the court, he was not exactly a model employee. In the span of just over a month in 2019, Waiters was suspended twice by the team. The first time, Waiters ingested edibles laced with THC, had a panic attack, and missed a team flight along with his upcoming game. The second time, Waiters reported an illness but then uploaded photos of himself partying on a boat to social media.

6. Heat shooting guard Steve Smith once sank seven three-pointers in a single NBA quarter and remains one of just three players ever to do so.

7. Just one point guard who has played for the Heat has been enshrined in the Basketball Hall of Fame: Gary Payton, who was elected in 2013.

8. The streetball stylings of Heat point guard Rafer Alston made him famous well before Alston entered the NBA. As a member of the And1 Mixtape Tour in 1999, Alston's dazzling moves and flashy style earned him many fans who were eventually delighted to see his game transition successfully to the professional court.

9. Miami guard Anthony Carter was a bench player with the team who lost nearly $3 million in 2003 when his agent forgot to notify the Heat that Carter wanted to exercise his player option. Rather than fire the agent, Carter stuck with him, signed for the league minimum with the San

Antonio Spurs, and waited two decades for the agent to slowly pay back the money his mistake had lost Carter.

10. Heat forward Justise Winslow comes from good bloodlines. His father, Rickie Winslow, was a player at the University of Houston during the famous "Phi Slamma Jamma" years alongside Hall-of-Famers Clyde Drexler and Hakeem Olajuwon. Justise edged his father in NBA Draft position though, 10th overall to 28th.

CHAPTER 9:

CENTERS OF ATTENTION

QUIZ TIME!

1. Where was champion Heat center Shaquille O'Neal born?

    a. New Orleans, Louisiana

    b. Miami, Florida

    c. Newark, New Jersey

    d. San Diego, California

2. Miami center Stephane Lasme is the only Heat player who hails from the country of Gabon.

    a. True

    b. False

3. Heat big man Sean Marks was the first player ever to reach the NBA who was born in which country?

    a. Sudan

    b. Argentina

    c. Indonesia

    d. New Zealand

4. Center Shaquille O'Neal was a key member of the 2006 championship team in Miami, but he also won three NBA titles with which other franchise?

   a. Orlando Magic
   b. Boston Celtics
   c. Los Angeles Lakers
   d. Cleveland Cavaliers

5. Outgoing Miami center Shaquille O'Neal also released six rap albums in his spare time. Which of these albums became a platinum-selling hit record?

   a. Shaq Fu: Da Return
   b. Shaq Diesel
   c. You Can't Stop the Reign
   d. Shoot Pass Slam!

6. Which of the following is NOT a fact about eclectic Heat center Rony Seikaly?

   a. He speaks four languages: English, French, Greek, and Arabic.
   b. He played for four NBA teams: Miami, Golden State, Orlando, and New Jersey.
   c. He owns four Miami restaurants: Sosta, Solea, Quattro, and Club Wall.
   d. He has been married to four models: Elsa Benitez, Martha Graeff, Cindy Kouzopoulis, and Ana Ribeiro.

7. Miami center Jamaal Magloire had a half-brother named Justin Sheppard who was also a basketball player, but

Sheppard was killed at 19 years old in a murder that has yet to be solved.

   a. True

   b. False

8. Although popular center Amar'e Stoudemire fell a little bit short of leading the Miami Heat to a championship, he did win titles with two different squads in which league after his NBA career finished?

   a. Novo Basquete Brasil

   b. Basketball Bundesliga (Germany)

   c. Israeli Basketball Premier League

   d. Lega Basket Serie A (Italy)

9. Which aging center joined Miami in 2010 as a useful but less heralded free-agent addition along with forward LeBron James and center Chris Bosh?

   a. Patrick Ewing

   b. Dikembe Mutombo

   c. Shawn Bradley

   d. Zydrunas Ilgauskas

10. What was the name given to the strategy that opposing teams used to slow down Heat center Shaquille O'Neal, who was a notoriously bad free-throw shooter?

   a. The O'Neal Oh No

   b. Distract Da-Shaq

   c. The Hack-a-Shaq

   d. The Brick Layer

11. Heat center Hassan Whiteside is the son of Hasson Arbubakrr, another excellent athlete who played professionally with which two teams?

    a. The National Basketball Association's Detroit Pistons and Houston Rockets
    b. Major League Baseball's Baltimore Orioles and Seattle Mariners
    c. The National Hockey League's Calgary Flames and Buffalo Sabres
    d. The National Football League's Minnesota Vikings and Tampa Bay Buccaneers

12. Miami pivot Bam Adebayo led the NBA in field goal percentage in just his second season in the league.

    a. True
    b. False

13. What is the name of the radio show that former Heat center (and experienced DJ) Rony Seikaly hosts on Sirius/XM in his retirement?

    a. Sugar Free Radio
    b. The Heat Index
    c. Rockin' with Rony
    d. The Sweet Sounds of Seikaly

14. In 2016, Miami pivot Hassan Whiteside became the first player in NBA history to do which of the following?

    a. Record 20 points and 20 rebounds in a game in which he came off the bench rather than starting

b. Transition from making the league's minimum possible salary to maximum level earnings under the salary cap

c. Achieve a double-double in every single game during the regular season

d. Win the NBA's Sixth Man of the Year Award and Most Valuable Player trophy in the same season

15. Which of the following statements about popular Heat center Chris Bosh is NOT true?

a. He was forced to retire early from the NBA due to dangerous blood clots.

b. He has his own YouTube channel with tens of thousands of subscribers.

c. He has his jersey number retired with two different NBA franchises.

d. He is a member of the National Society of Black Engineers.

16. No Heat center has ever led the team in points scored during a single game.

a. True

b. False

17. Which of the following statements is NOT true about iconic Heat center Alonzo Mourning?

a. In retirement, he became the Heat's vice president of player programs and development, focusing on reaching out to young players in the Miami community.

b. The city of Miami named a high school after him and his wife, the Alonzo and Tracy Mourning Senior High Biscayne Bay Campus.

c. He played basketball at the White House in a game held to celebrate President Barack Obama's 50th birthday.

d. Through various charities, including his own, Zo's Fund for Life, Mourning has donated over $600 million.

18. The Heat's first franchise player, center Rony Seikaly, was also one of the first NBA stars born outside the United States of America. In which country was Seikaly born?

   a. Greece
   b. Lebanon
   c. Turkey
   d. Israel

19. Which Heat center was the franchise leader in points, blocks, rebounds, and minutes on the court for another team before coming to Miami?

   a. Alonzo Mourning for the Charlotte Hornets
   b. Jermaine O'Neal for the Indiana Pacers
   c. Chris Bosh for the Toronto Raptors
   d. Shaquille O'Neal for the Orlando Magic

20. Miami center Matt Geiger owned a 28,000-square-foot mansion that was the biggest in his Florida county. The building was so remarkable that it was used as a setting in

the comic book movie *The Punisher,* featuring John Travolta.

a. True
b. False

QUIZ ANSWERS

1. C – Newark, New Jersey

2. A – True

3. D – New Zealand

4. C – Los Angeles Lakers

5. B – *Shaq Diesel*

6. D – He has been married to four models: Elsa Benitez, Martha Graeff, Cindy Kouzopoulis, and Ana Ribeiro.

7. A – True

8. C – Israeli Basketball Premier League

9. D – Zydrunas Ilgauskas

10. C – The Hack-a-Shaq

11. D – The National Football League's Minnesota Vikings and Tampa Bay Buccaneers

12. B – False

13. A – *Sugar Free Radio*

14. B – Transition from making the league's minimum possible salary to maximum level earnings under the salary cap

15. C – He has his jersey number retired with two different NBA franchises.

16. B – False

17. D – Through various charities, including his own, Zo's Fund For Life, Mourning has donated over $600 million.

18. B – Lebanon

19. C – Chris Bosh for the Toronto Raptors

20. A – True

DID YOU KNOW?

1. Miami big man Matt Geiger was noted throughout his NBA career for his seven-foot stature and shaved head. While the look was fierce, the reasoning behind it was not. Geiger shaved his head in support of his twin brother, Mark, who had suffered from Hodgkin's disease.

2. In a touching gesture of support, Heat center Rony Seikaly volunteered to play a one-on-one matchup against Los Angeles Lakers superstar Magic Johnson after Johnson was diagnosed as HIV positive, and many in the NBA feared allowing him to return to play.

3. Before Canadian center Kelly Olynyk made it to the NBA as a big man with the Miami Heat, another member of his family beat him to the big leagues. Olynyk's mother, Arlene, was the NBA's first female scorekeeper. She served in that position with the Toronto Raptors from 1995 to 2004.

4. After his NBA career finished, Heat pivot Isaac Austin invested in a team called the Utah Snowbears in the American Basketball Association. Austin chose to coach the team himself, and the Snowbears were rolling with a 27-1 record when Austin became angry about the league's refereeing and forfeited the playoffs out of principle. He eventually folded the team altogether because of the disagreement.

5. Center Michael Doleac earned a championship with the Miami Heat in 2006 and shortly afterward went back to school at the University of Utah and earned a master's degree in physics. Doleac then became a high school physics teacher and basketball coach.

6. During his rookie season in the NBA, future Heat center Shaquille O'Neal twice dunked the ball so powerfully that it destroyed the backboard, causing the NBA to strengthen their design after the season.

7. Many players put on weight after their playing career ends, but Heat big man Dexter Pittman did the opposite. Pittman weighed as much as 388 pounds as a high school player and worked hard throughout his college years to get down to a healthier playing weight, which hovers around 100 pounds lower than that.

8. The first Chinese-born athlete to play in the NBA, center Wang Zhizhi, suited up for Miami from 2003 to 2005. Zhizhi averaged 2.5 points per game, so his cultural contributions outweighed his performance, and he returned to China after that stint.

9. Heat center Amar'e Stoudemire explored a wide swath of business opportunities during and after his time playing for Miami. Among other things, Stoudemire has performed in several television shows and movies, started his own record label, developed his own clothing line, written children's books, and created a wine label.

10. Though center Shaquille O'Neal was a bona fide superstar and MVP candidate, he came to Miami to chase a championship, rather than stats. O'Neal made this very clear to the media, saying, "Stats don't matter. I care about winning, not stats. If I score zero points and we win, I'm happy."

CHAPTER 10:

THE FORWARDS

QUIZ TIME!

1. Forward Martin Muursepp is the only player ever born in which country to play, not just for the Miami Heat, but in the NBA?

   a. Latvia
   b. Estonia
   c. Belarus
   d. Yemen

2. Heat forward Keith Askins, who played nine years with the team, was born and raised in Miami, Florida.

   a. True
   b. False

3. About which Heat forward did an NBA general manager say, "His story is one of the most remarkable I've seen in all my years of basketball. There were so many times in his life where he was set up to fail. Every time, he overcame just enormous odds."?

a. Grant Long

b. Udonis Haslem

c. Glen Rice

d. Jimmy Butler

4. Which of the following is NOT a fact about Miami Heat forward Lamar Odom?

a. Odom was once found unconscious in a brothel in Nevada and spent time in a coma recovering in a hospital afterward.

b. Odom was the owner of four tattoo parlors in Miami and its surrounding counties during his time with the Heat.

c. Odom was married to television personality Khloe Kardashian and appeared frequently on her reality series Keeping Up with the Kardashians before the two started their own reality series.

d. Odom started his own production company to enter the film industry and called it Rich Soil Entertainment.

5. The initials in popular Heat forward KZ Okpala's name are short for what?

a. Kevin Zachary

b. Kemba Zaire

c. Chikezie

d. Nothing; KZ is his given name.

6. In 2008, future Heat forward LeBron James became the first black man to appear on the cover of which publication?

a. Cigar Aficionado magazine

b. *Playboy* magazine

c. Hockey News magazine

d. *Vogue* magazine

7. Despite earning over $108 million during his NBA playing days, Heat power forward Antoine Walker filed for bankruptcy just two years after leaving the league.

   a. True

   b. False

8. Which Miami forward was easily identifiable by his signature looks, including a Mohawk hairstyle and tattoos on over half of his body, including arms, legs, hands, chest, back, and neck?

   a. Antony Mason

   b. Chris Bosh

   c. Dan Majerle

   d. Chris Anderson

9. Which two former Miami Heat forwards competed as a duo on the popular reality television series *The Amazing Race*?

   a. Shawn Marion and Cedric Ceballos

   b. Glen Rice and Antoine Walker

   c. Lamar Odom and James Jones

   d. Shane Battier and Caron Butler

10. Heat forward LeBron James was the first player in NBA history to accomplish which of the following athletic feats?

a. Play all five positions during an NBA playoff game

b. Win an NBA championship with three different franchises

c. Record a triple-double against every franchise in the NBA

d. Be named All-Star Game Most Valuable Player in both the Eastern and Western Conferences

11. Which of the following is NOT a fact about Heat forward Caron Butler?

a. He has an addiction to the soft drink Mountain Dew, admitting to drinking up to half a dozen per day.

b. He owns six franchises of the restaurant Burger King after having worked there in his youth.

c. His autobiography *Tuff Juice: My Journey from the Streets to the NBA* is set to become a movie, with Mark Wahlberg serving as executive producer.

d. He loves to snowboard and once competed in a trick contest against Olympic snowboarder Shaun White.

12. His longest stint was three years with the Miami Heat because forward Earl Barron was a basketball nomad, spending time playing for 22 professional teams across 14 seasons and several different countries.

a. True

b. False

13. From which of his many non-basketball-related hobbies did Heat forward Earl Barron earn over $10,000?

a. Selling model trains that Barron builds himself

b. Creating musically enhanced recordings for people's voicemail messages

c. Playing cards at the World Series of Poker

d. Playing *League of Legends* at esports tournaments

14. Miami forward P.J. Brown endeared himself to Heat fans (and earned a suspension) when he picked up and tossed which New York Knicks guard on top of a group of photographers seated along the court?

a. John Starks

b. Chris Childs

c. Stephon Marbury

d. Charlie Ward

15. Which of the following media releases did Heat forward Juwan Howard NOT participate in at some point during his life?

a. The feature film *Hoop Dreams*

b. The rap song "It's Time to Ball"

c. The bestselling book *The Da Vinci Code*

d. The television show *The West Wing*

16. Respected forward Shane Battier is the only NBA player to have been on two different teams that posted winning streaks of 20 games or more: 22 in a row with the Houston Rockets and 27 in a row with the Miami Heat.

a. True

b. False

17. Which of the following is NOT a fact about Miami Heat small forward Jimmy Butler?

   a. He appeared in a country music video by Luke Bryan called "Light It Up."
   b. He went on a vacation in Paris with actor Mark Wahlberg, whom he considers a friend.
   c. He operated a coffee shop in the NBA Bubble during the COVID-19 pandemic.
   d. He proposed to his girlfriend while stuck on the Space Mountain ride at Walt Disney World.

18. Heat forward Anthony Mason was a favorite player of the rap group the Beastie Boys. Mason not only appeared in a video for their song "Root Down," but was also immortalized in which of the following lyrics on the track "B-Boys Makin' with the Freak Freak"?

   a. "I got my hair cut correct like Anthony Mason/Then I ride the IRT right up to Penn Station"
   b. "Try to blow past me, I'll reject you like Mase/Shove the ball back at you right into your face"
   c. "Stable and solid and ready for chasin'/Dominatin' the rap game like I'm Anthony Mason"
   d. "She wouldn't believe all the troubles I'm facin'/Gotta stare 'em down hard just like Anthony Mason"

19. Which Heat forward was born in the Bronx, New York, and learned his basketball skills at the famous Rucker Park, which was within walking distance from his home?

   a. Glen Rice
   b. Jamal Mashburn

c. Shawn Marion

d. Kendall Gill

20. Miami small forward Shane Battier is the only basketball player ever to be named both Naismith Prep Player of the Year and Naismith College Player of the Year.

   a. True

   b. False

QUIZ ANSWERS

1. B – Estonia

2. B – False

3. D – Jimmy Butler

4. B – Odom was the owner of four tattoo parlors in Miami and its surrounding counties during his time with the Heat.

5. C – Chikezie

6. D – *Vogue* magazine

7. A – True

8. D – Chris Anderson

9. A – Shawn Marion and Cedric Ceballos

10. C – Record a triple-double against every franchise in the NBA

11. D – He loves to snowboard, and once competed in a trick contest against Olympic snowboarder Shaun White.

12. A – True

13. C – Playing cards at the World Series of Poker

14. D – Charlie Ward

15. C – The bestselling book *The Da Vinci Code*

16. A – True

17. D – He proposed to his girlfriend while stuck on the Space Mountain ride at Walt Disney World.

18. A – "I got my hair cut correct like Anthony Mason/Then I ride the IRT right up to Penn Station"

19. B – Jamal Mashburn

20. A – True

DID YOU KNOW?

1. Forward Michael Beasley, who had three stints with Miami, was really attached to the name Michael and its derivatives. His father was Michael Sr., his sister was Mychaela, and he named his son and daughter Michael III and Mikaiya.

2. After his playing career ended, Heat power forward Brian Grant was diagnosed with Parkinson's disease. Grant partnered with other celebrities who suffered from the disease, including legendary boxer Muhammad Ali and iconic actor Michael J. Fox, to start the Brian Grant Foundation, which works to support those who have Parkinson's.

3. Miami power forward Kevin Willis carved out an incredible 21-season NBA career, which is tied for second place all-time behind only Vince Carter's 22 seasons. After retiring, the seven-foot, 245-pound Willis devoted his time to working with his clothing company that produces stylish offerings for big and tall men, Willis & Walker.

4. In 2019, former Heat forward LeBron James filed a request for a trademark of the term "Taco Tuesday" after posting pictures of his family's Mexican dishes on the social media platform Instagram. The United States Patent and Trademark Office turned down James's application on the grounds that the term was too commonly used.

5. Power forward Joel Anthony won two championships with the Heat, making him one of the most successful Canadian NBA players in history. Anthony is behind only center Bill Wennington and forward Rick Fox, who won three titles each as members of the Chicago Bulls and Los Angeles Lakers, respectively.

6. Only two NBA teammates in league history have recorded triple-doubles in the same game together on more than one occasion. That would be current Heat forward duo Jimmy Butler and Bam Adebayo.

7. After moving from the Heat to the Philadelphia 76ers in 1994, forward Willie Burton torched Miami with 53 points when he faced his former team. Burton achieved this on only 19 shots, giving him the NBA record for fewest attempts needed to break the 50-point barrier.

8. Miami forward James Johnson is a noted martial artist. Johnson reached black belt level in karate, competed in MMA, and owns an undefeated 20-0 record in kickboxing.

9. After his retirement, Heat forward Jamal Mashburn continued to live in Miami and diversified his investment portfolio. Mashburn owns multiple car dealerships, 34 Outback Steakhouses, and 37 Papa John's, as well as shares in a racehorse stable.

10. Power forward Udonis Haslem has been with the Miami Heat since 2003. Haslem no longer plays often, but his 18 years with the team is the longest current tenure of any NBA player. Steph Curry is second on the list; Curry has

played for the Golden State Warriors since 2009. Haslem's tenure is tied for fifth all-time.

CHAPTER 11:

COACHES, GMS, & OWNERS

QUIZ TIME!

1. Who served as the Heat's first general manager?

    a. Randy Pfund

    b. Lewis Schaffel

    c. Pat Riley

    d. Ted Arison

2. No Heat head coach has lasted more than a decade in the position before retiring or being fired.

    a. True

    b. False

3. The Heat's first head coach, Ron Rothstein, lasted for how long in that position with the franchise?

    a. 46 games

    b. 1 season

    c. 3 seasons

    d. 8 seasons

4. The Heat's most recent coach, Erik Spoelstra, got his start in the coaching ranks in which basketball league?

    a. NCAA
    b. Bundesliga
    c. Serie A
    d. NBA G League

5. Miami Heat founder Ted Arison amassed his fortune primarily as the founder of which two companies?

    a. Norwegian Cruise Lines and Carnival Cruise Lines
    b. Cineplex Odeon Theaters and IMAX Theaters
    c. Domino's Pizza and Waffle House
    d. Sprint Telecommunications and Verizon Telecommunications

6. Of all the Miami bench bosses who have coached over 100 NBA games with the team, which one had the lowest winning percentage at only .232?

    a. Ron Rothstein
    b. Stan Van Gundy
    c. Kevin Loughery
    d. Erik Spoelstra

7. Miami is the only NBA franchise to have a player rise from playing for the team to ownership of the team.

    a. True
    b. False

8. Which coach led the Heat to their first NBA championship?

a. Stan Van Gundy

b. Erik Spoelstra

c. Pat Riley

d. Alvin Gentry

9. Which Miami general manager once took the floor as a player on the team before getting the chance to guide it from the front office?

a. Dave Wohl

b. Pat Riley

c. Randy Pfund

d. No Heat GM has ever played for the team.

10. Who is the Miami leader in all-time coaching wins with the franchise?

a. Stan Van Gundy

b. Pat Riley

c. Ron Rothstein

d. Erik Spoelstra

11. Which Hall of Fame basketball player was one of the original minority owners of the Miami Heat?

a. Center Moses Malone

b. Forward Julius Erving

c. Forward Billy Cunningham

d. Guard Jerry West

12. Heat coach Stan Van Gundy has a brother named Jeff, who coached the rival New York Knicks and the Houston Rockets.

a. True

b. False

13. How many of the Heat's six head coaches have spent their entire NBA coaching career with Miami?

    a. 0

    b. 1

    c. 3

    d. 6

14. Which Heat general manager has led the franchise to the fewest playoff appearances?

    a. Randy Pfund

    b. Pat Riley

    c. Lewis Schaffel

    d. Dave Wohl

15. In four seasons coaching the Heat, how many times did coach Kevin Loughery finish above .500?

    a. 1

    b. 2

    c. 3

    d. 4

16. At one point in their history, the Heat employed four coaches over a decade who had all started for Miami at some point during their playing careers.

    a. True

    b. False

17. How did Micky Arison become the majority owner of the Miami Heat in 1995?

    a. He purchased the team when the previous owners wished to sell.
    b. He inherited the team from his father.
    c. He forced a takeover of the corporation that had previously owned the team.
    d. He was hired as CEO of the company that owned the team.

18. Which of the following is NOT a fact about Miami Heat coach and team president Pat Riley?

    a. He was the first person in any North American sport to win a championship as a player, assistant coach, head coach, and executive.
    b. He was a National Football League draft pick of the Dallas Cowboys at the wide receiver position.
    c. He has participated in the NBA Finals in some capacity in six different decades.
    d. He was brought in as a minority owner of the Heat after his 20th season with the franchise.

19. Which Heat coach is the only one of the following to have won the NBA Coach of the Year Award while behind the bench for Miami?

    a. Kevin Loughery
    b. Erik Spoelstra
    c. Pat Riley
    d. Stan Van Gundy

20. Heat owner Micky Arison once proposed trading franchises with New York Yankees owner George Steinbrenner as part of a business deal.

    a. True
    b. False

QUIZ ANSWERS

1. B – Lewis Schaffel

2. B – False

3. C – 3 seasons

4. B – Bundesliga

5. A – Norwegian Cruise Lines and Carnival Cruise Lines

6. A – Ron Rothstein

7. B – False

8. C – Pat Riley

9. D – No Heat GM has ever played for the team.

10. D – Erik Spoelstra

11. C – Forward Billy Cunningham

12. A – True

13. B – 1

14. C – Lewis Schaffel

15. A – 1

16. B – False

17. B – He inherited the team from his father.

18. D – He was brought in as a minority owner of the Heat after his 20th season with the franchise.

19. C – Pat Riley

20. B – False

DID YOU KNOW?

1. Heat minority owner Billy Cunningham had an excellent basketball career in his own right. Cunningham won an NBA championship alongside legend Wilt Chamberlain, made the All-NBA first team three times, had his number retired by the Philadelphia 76ers, and was named to the NBA's 50th Anniversary All-Time Team.

2. Only one man has served as both coach and general manager of the Miami Heat. Pat Riley coached the team for 849 games in two stints with the team and has handled the personnel duties for the past 12 years after moving up from behind the bench.

3. Miami founder Ted Arison enlisted in the British Army's Jewish Brigade and battled against the Nazis in World War II, fighting mostly in Italy, before working with the Israeli military afterward.

4. Heat general managers Randy Pfund and Pat Riley both got their start as assistant coaches in the Los Angeles Lakers organization. When Riley became the head coach, he hired Pfund as his assistant and both men eventually ended up with Miami.

5. The Heat's rivalry with the New York Knicks was heightened in 1995 when Knicks coach Pat Riley gave up his position to become Miami's coach and team president

instead. The Knicks claimed Miami had tampered with Riley, and the Heat was forced to pay $1 million and give up a 1st round draft pick, but the move was worth it, as Riley remains with the team to this day.

6. Although both Ted and Micky Arison, owners of the Heat, were born in Israel, none of the top executives for the Heat have ever been born outside of the United States.

7. Current Heat owner Micky Arison owns not one, but two yachts that serve as homes for him. The "Sirona III" stretches 185 feet and the "Mylin IV" is 200 feet long.

8. Miami GM Dave Wohl plied his trade as an assistant coach in addition to becoming an executive. Wohl coached for nine different NBA organizations, including Miami, New Jersey, Milwaukee, Orlando, Sacramento, Boston, Minnesota, and both the Los Angeles Lakers and Clippers.

9. The Heat have never had a head coach who was born outside the United States. They have also never had a coach who was born in Miami. In fact, three of the six coaches in franchise history were born in New York, including Kevin Loughery, Ron Rothstein, and Pat Riley.

10. Once in league history, a Miami general manager has been awarded the NBA Executive of the Year Award. Pat Riley received the honor in 2010-11 when the team won the Southeast division title and progressed to the NBA Finals.

CHAPTER 12:

THE AWARDS SECTION

QUIZ TIME!

1. Who is the only player to have won the most Maurice Podoloff Trophies as league MVP while playing for Miami, earning the hardware twice?

   a. Guard Dwyane Wade

   b. Center Alonzo Mourning

   c. Center Shaquille O'Neal

   d. Forward LeBron James

2. The first Heat player to win any major award given out by the NBA was franchise guard Dwyane Wade.

   a. True

   b. False

3. During which season did the Heat win its first Larry O'Brien Trophy as NBA champions?

   a. 1998-99

   b. 2002-03

c. 2005-06

d. 2010-11

4. In 1996, the NBA announced its 50 Greatest Players in NBA history. How many of these players ever suited up for the Heat?

    a. 0
    b. 1
    c. 6
    d. 9

5. The J. Walter Kennedy Trophy, given to an NBA player who shows "great service and dedication to the community," has been awarded to which Heat player(s)?

    a. Guard Dwyane Wade in 2009-10
    b. Guard Mario Chalmers in 1997-98 and forward Jimmy Butler in 2019-20
    c. Guard Bimbo Coles in 1992-93
    d. Center Alonzo Mourning in 2001-02 and forward P.J. Brown in 1996-97

6. Which Heat player or players have won the Twyman-Stokes Trophy as NBA Teammate of the Year thanks to "selfless play and commitment and dedication to his team"?

    a. Forward P.J. Brown
    b. Forward Hassan Whiteside
    c. Forward Shane Battier
    d. Center Rony Seikaly

7. In the team's illustrious history, no Miami Heat player has ever led the NBA in rebounding for a season.

    a. True
    b. False

8. Who was the Miami player to make the NBA All-Rookie first team most recently?

    a. Guard Kendrick Nunn
    b. Guard Tyler Herro
    c. Forward Justise Winslow
    d. Forward Michael Beasley

9. Which Heat player or players have won the NBA All-Star Game MVP Award while representing Miami?

    a. Center Alonzo Mourning and guard Steve Smith
    b. Centers Alonzo Mourning, Shaquille O'Neal, and guard Dwyane Wade
    c. Forward LeBron James and guard Tim Hardaway
    d. Guard Dwyane Wade

10. Which of these Heat icons is the only one to finish a season as the league's leading scorer while playing for Miami?

    a. Center Shaquille O'Neal
    b. Forward LeBron James
    c. Guard Dwyane Wade
    d. Forward Glen Rice

11. The Sixth Man of the Year Award for best performing player as a substitute has been won by how many Heat players in franchise history?

    a. 0
    b. 2
    c. 3
    d. 5

12. Heat center Shaquille O'Neal auctioned off his Miami Heat 2005-06 championship ring for charity on eBay in 2016. The ring fetched $2.1 million, which O'Neal donated to a relief fund for victims of Hurricane Matthew who lived in the Miami area.

    a. True
    b. False

13. Two-time Slam Dunk Contest champion Harold Miner of the Miami Heat faced off multiple times against which other event winner in the contest during the mid-1990s?

    a. Brent Barry of the Los Angeles Clippers
    b. Isaiah Rider of the Minnesota Timberwolves
    c. Dee Brown of the Boston Celtics
    d. Kobe Bryant of the Los Angeles Lakers

14. Of the Heat players in the Basketball Hall of Fame, center Alonzo Mourning was the first among them to play with Miami. What year did he begin playing with the team?

    a. 1995-96
    b. 1997-98

c. 2000-01

d. 2002-03

15. Which Heat player has been selected to the most NBA All-Star Games while playing for Miami?

a. Forward LeBron James

b. Center Shaquille O'Neal

c. Forward Udonis Haslem

d. Guard Dwyane Wade

16. No Miami Heat player has ever won the Eddie Gottlieb Trophy as the league's top rookie.

a. True

b. False

17. Four different Miami Heat players (Jason Kapono, James Jones, Glen Rice, and Daequan Cook) have won the NBA's Three-Point Contest, tying the Heat with which other two franchises for the most victories in that event?

a. Golden State Warriors and Sacramento Kings

b. Cleveland Cavaliers and Phoenix Suns

c. Boston Celtics and Chicago Bulls

d. Portland Trail Blazers and Utah Jazz

18. Who was the Miami player to make the NBA All-Defensive first team most recently?

a. Guard Dwyane Wade

b. Forward Hassan Whiteside

c. Center Bam Adebayo

d. Forward LeBron James

19. In which year did Miami host the NBA's annual All-Star Game, despite not having any players represented on the team?

    a. 1990
    b. 1995
    c. 2000
    d. 2005

20. For almost two decades, computer company IBM gave an award to the NBA player judged by its programming formulas to be most valuable to his team. Center Shaquille O'Neal received the award twice while playing for Miami.

    a. True
    b. False

QUIZ ANSWERS

1. D – Forward LeBron James

2. B – False

3. C – 2005-06

4. B – 1

5. D – Center Alonzo Mourning in 2001-02 and forward P.J. Brown in 1996-97

6. C – Forward Shane Battier

7. B – False

8. A – Guard Kendrick Nunn

9. D – Guard Dwyane Wade

10. C – Guard Dwyane Wade

11. A – 0

12. B – False

13. B – Isaiah Rider of the Minnesota Timberwolves

14. A – 1995-96

15. D – Guard Dwyane Wade

16. A – True

17. C – Boston Celtics and Chicago Bulls

18. D – Forward LeBron James

19. A – 1990

20. B – False

DID YOU KNOW?

1. The Joe Dumars Trophy for sportsmanship, ethical behavior, fair play, and integrity has never been won by a Heat player, although some winners, such as forward P.J. Brown and guard Steve Smith, did play for Miami at other points during their careers.

2. Each year, the NBA denotes three teams' worth of All-NBA players, and the Heat has been well represented. Guard Tim Hardaway was the first Heat player to appear, making it three times in a row from 1996-97 to 1998-99, while teammate Alonzo Mourning made appearances in the last two of those seasons.

3. Only four players have earned the NBA's relatively new Lifetime Achievement Award. No Heat players have been named, but that is unsurprising, given the team's comparatively recent entry into the NBA.

4. When the NBA announced the top 10 teams in its history in 1996, the Heat had been in existence for less than a decade. Only three teams made the list from after Miami's entrance into the league and none of them were Heat teams.

5. Coach Pat Riley built the Miami Heat into a defensive force in the late 1990s. His success was easily demonstrated when center Alonzo Mourning won back-

to-back NBA Defensive Player of the Year Awards in 1998-99 and 1999-2000.

6. One unusual award was given to Heat center Alonzo Mourning in 2015. The Library of Virginia (Mourning's birth state) honored him as one of its "Strong Men and Women in Virginia History" thanks to his philanthropy and basketball career.

7. Twice in NBA history, a Miami Heat player has won the Most Improved Player Award. Both players were centers: Rony Seikaly won the award in 1989-90, and Isaac Austin won it in 1996-97.

8. The original Miami Heat winner of the Bill Russell Trophy as NBA Finals Most Valuable Player was guard Dwyane Wade in 2006. Forward LeBron James surpassed Wade though, winning the award back to back in 2012 and 2013.

9. The Heat featured three winners of the NBA All-Star Weekend Slam Dunk Contest. High flying guard Harold Miner won the title twice, in 1993 and 1995. The most recent contest in 2020 was also won by a Heat player, young forward Derrick Jones Jr.

10. USA Basketball names its top male basketball player in international competition each year. Heat center Alonzo Mourning pulled off an incredible feat, winning this award twice, a full decade apart, in 1990 and 2000.

CONCLUSION

There you have it; an amazing collection of Miami Heat trivia, information, and statistics at your fingertips! Regardless of how you fared on the quizzes, we hope that you found this book entertaining, enlightening, and educational.

Ideally, you knew many of these details but also learned a good deal more about the history of the Miami Heat, their players, coaches, management, and some of the quirky stories surrounding the team. If you got a little peek into the colorful details that make being a fan so much more enjoyable, then mission accomplished!

The good news is that the trivia doesn't have to stop there! Spread the word. Challenge your fellow Heat fans to see if they can do any better. Share some of the stories with the next generation to help them become Miami supporters, too.

If you are a big enough Heat fan, consider creating your own quiz with some of the details you know that weren't presented here and then test your friends to see if they can match your knowledge.

The Miami Heat is a storied franchise with a long history that includes multiple periods of success and a few periods that were less than successful. They've had glorious superstars, iconic moments, hilarious tales...but most of all, they have wonderful, passionate fans. Thank you for being one of them.

Made in the USA
Columbia, SC
18 May 2024

35863654R00075